C# Programming For Beginners & Intermediates

C# Made Easy Step By Step With Hands-on Projects

Craig Berg

Your Gift

Let me help you master this and other programming languages quickly.

Visit

https://bit.ly/codetutorials

To Find Out More

Introduction

You Are About To Learn How To Step And Dive Into The Shallow And Deep Waters Of C# Programming, With Confidence!

There are many reasons why you need to learn programming today, and even more reasons why you need to learn programming with C#.

If you want to ***boost your own problem solving ability***, ***explore your creativity*** and ***become an innovator***, ***accelerate your career*** as you help fill or meet the global demand for software developers or *even* ***boost your business***, you should definitely learn programming.

However, if you want to ***accelerate your understanding of coding*** and get started fast, ***gain access to many toolsets*** backed by Microsoft, ***enjoy more flexibility*** in terms of the applications you can develop with C#, ***work with a popular and well-supported language***, then C# is what you need.

Yes, C# is the 4th most popular programming language and has the 3rd largest community on StackOverflow (the platform which was also built using C#). What's more, it is considered cleaner than Java and much more modern than Python, and other programming languages. It is no wonder considered to be the universal language of programming, which perhaps explains why you are here!

Perhaps you are wondering...

How does C# compare with other programming languages like Python, Java and others?

Why should I learn C#; is it still relevant in 2020 and beyond?

Where do I start when learning C#?

What core concepts do I need to learn to create my first program?

How to I master such things like variables, data types, conditional statements, objects, classes, loops, strings, lists and arrays in C#?

If you have these and other related questions, this book is for you, so keep reading.

More precisely, this book will teach you:

- What C# programming language is, and why it's the best languages for beginners and intermediates
- **How to install the program in your PC irrespective of your operating system and set up the environment to work with**
- How to understand and work with C# variables
- **How to understand and work with different types of data and operators in C#**
- How to work with conditional statements for decision making in C#
- **Why objects and classes are important in C#, and how you can create your own**
- How to create and work with loops in C#, and why you need them
- **How to handle strings, lists and arrays in C#**
- How to create your first project in C# in simple steps

..And so much more!

Yes, this book is here to take you through C# from the basics to the depths of the language whether you are new to this or an intermediate in an incredibly simple tone, structure and language to ensure that in just a few days, you can create your first program.

So, if you've been struggling to figure out how to start coding or advance your programming skill because, perhaps from experience, you think the whole thing is difficult, or because you've never found that one "ultimate guide" to give you thorough, step-by-step directions and make sure you not only move fast, but "get" everything, you now have what you've been looking for.

Your desire and quest to get an excellent guide has finally paid off.

Let's begin!

Table of Contents

Introduction to C# Programming & The .Net Framework

C#, pronounced as c-sharp or see-sharp, is a high-level, robust, and modern programming language. C# is also a simple object-oriented programming language that exists within the .NET family of programming languages. It was developed by Microsoft under the .NET initiative led by Anders Hejlsberg, author of Turbo Pascal and Delphi, both of which are famous programming languages in their own right.

Like most programming languages, C# came about as an improvement over other programming languages, especially the ones that had come before it, such as C++, C, and the Java programming language. Because of this, C# may have a syntax that seems familiar to that of C, C++, and the Java programming language with a slight difference in certain cases.

C# allows developers to create secure and robust applications for desktop, mobile, server, embedded systems, and web. In this book, we are going to cover the major concepts of the C# programming language in detail, and in a way that will help you understand C# in a unique and easy way so that as you continue your learning journey, you can understand deeper aspects of the language.

NOTE: This book is very beginners' and intermediates' friendly. As such, we may mention —but not explain— advanced topics of the C# language such as Generics, Delegates, Events, Lambda Expressions, LINQ, Nullable Types, Dynamics, and Asynchronous Programming. As you master the beginner and intermediate aspects of C#, make sure you seek out knowledge on the advanced topic mentioned above and others, and that you challenge yourself to learn as much about the language as possible.

PS: I'd like your feedback. If you are happy with this book, please leave a review on Amazon.

Please leave a review for this book on Amazon by visiting the page below:

https://amzn.to/2VMR5qr

Introduction to the .NET Framework

We have noted that C# is a programming language within the .NET family. If you are new to C# programming, you may be wondering, "what exactly is the.NET family and what does it entail?"

.NET is a very famous development platform —mainly well known to Windows desktop application developers, video game and back-end web developers. Simplified, .NET, pronounced as dot net, is a cross-platform and open-source developer platform used to develop robust applications for desktop use across multiple operating systems.

It encapsulates the development of applications ranging from desktop applications, web applications, mobile applications, and as mentioned, C# is very popular in the gaming developer community.

Languages under the .NET initiative include C#, F#, Visual Basic, and ASP.NET. Each of these languages are similar in the sense that each made improvement to the other, and each finds use in the creation of applications in different fields.

The .NET family of languages is also very popular because of its wide range of predefined class libraries that support both simple and complex programs, data structures for various applications such as databases, security, encryption, artificial intelligence, and more.

The .NET libraries are under the maintenance of the NuGet package manager that allows for the installation and update of these packages. Summarized, the .NET framework is a very advanced ecosystem of various programming languages that we cannot discuss here individually because C# is the primary focus of this guidebook.

Core Features of the C# Programming Language

Even though we now have many programming languages, C# has managed to relevant. This is because of a few reasons, key of which is the core features and functionalities of C#.

Let us discuss some of the core features that make C# a great programming language compared to other programming languages with similar applications.

- It is a high-level programming language
- It is modern and general-purpose
- It is very easy to learn
- It is part of the .NET framework
- Easy to use Generics
- It creates very secure and efficient programs
- It is cross platform
- Assembly Versioning
- Indexers

- It is designed for CLI – Common Language Infrastructure
- Automatic and Efficient Garbage Collection
- Delegation and Event Management

Now that you know what C# is and its many advantages over other programming languages used for similar development application, let us discuss how to set up your C# learning and working environment the right way.

Section 1

Setup and Installation

In this section, we are going to look at how to setup C# on your computer and start creating C# programs. Before we begin this environment installation, you need to meet a few requirements necessary for running the C# Integrated Development Environment (IDE). For compatibility issues and efficient execution of the programs, ensure that your computer meets the following requirements:

- A 1.8Ghz and higher Processor – Preferably a 64-bit processor
- Windows 7 Service Pack 1 and higher
- 4GB of RAM and above (6GB for better performance)
- Minimum Disk Space of at least 8GB to 210 GB depending on the features you want to be installed
- Microsoft .NET Framework 4.5 and higher
- For the initial setup, you need a relatively good internet speed.

These basic requirements can determine whether C# will run smoothly on your System or not. If you have the above requirements, we can begin.

How to install the .NET Framework

The very first action we are going to conduct is that of installing .NET Framework 4.5 and higher. In this book, we are going to use version 4.7.

To download the .NET framework, follow this link:

https://www.microsoft.com/en-us/download/details.aspx?id=55167

To begin the download, select your preferred language and click download. Once the download has completed, start the executable and begin the installation.

NOTE: If you are running updated versions of Microsoft Windows 8.1 and above, you may have .NET already installed and you can go ahead and cancel the installation. If case it is not, complete the installation.

Installing the IDE (C#)

Here, we are going to cover the installation of the C# IDE that contains a text editor and C# compiler binaries. We are going to use the Microsoft Visual Studio (MVS) as the IDE.

You can use a variety of MVS-environment alternatives such as Jetbrains, Rider, and Mono IDE but some of these may require a subscription, which is why this book does not cover these installations.

Microsoft Visual Studio runs on Windows and Mac only (as of 2019). If you are a Linux user, you can download the Mono IDE, which is a very great alternative.

To download the visual studio installer, go to the following addresses for Mac and Windows users respectively

https://visualstudio.microsoft.com/vs/mac/

https://visualstudio.microsoft.com/vs/

Download the free, Community Edition. In case of added features or commercial usage, you can purchase the Enterprise or Professional editions.

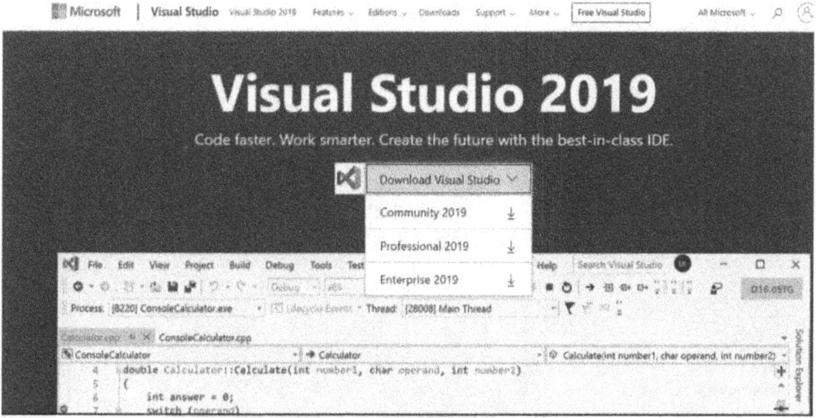

Once you get the installer, launch it, and wait until the initial setup completes and the visual studio installer launches.

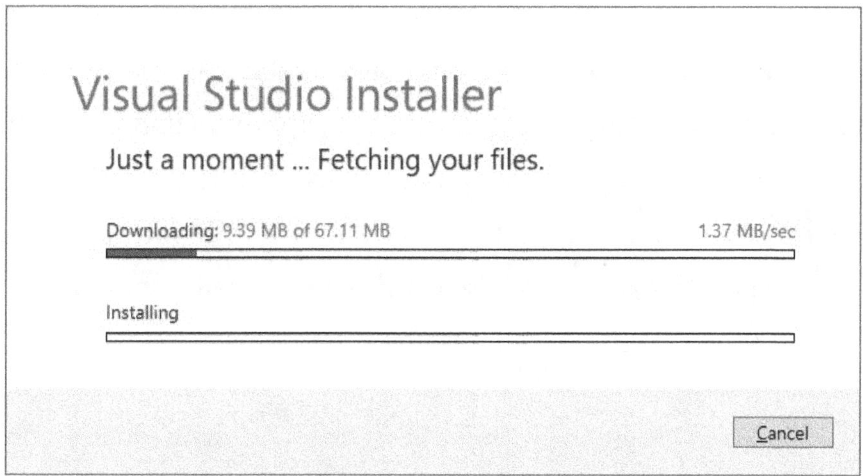

Once done, another window such as the one shown below shall open:

Select the community version and click install. Another window will launch requesting you to select the features to include during the IDE installation process. For this case, we require the .NET desktop environment. Select it and click install. If you would like to install additional features, select them but ensure you have the required space for the installation.

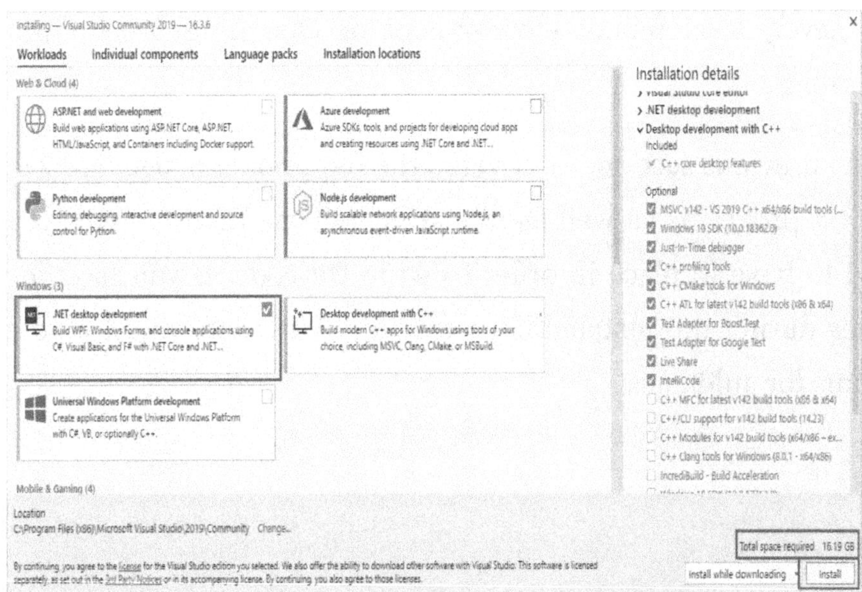

Once you have selected the features to install, click install for the installation to begin. Wait until the process completes and then launch it.

NOTE: In this book, we may interchange between Microsoft visual studio and Jetbrains Rider, but the code will work on whichever development environment or Operating System you are using.

In the previous section, we covered the requirements necessary to run C# programs as well as how to install the Environment you need to have in place in order to write C# code. If you face any issues during the installation, check out Microsoft visual studio forums for guidance.

Section 2

C# Basic Concepts

Hello World Program and Basic C# Program Structure

Before we discuss the foundational concepts of the C# programming language, let us look at how to create the most basic C# Program. By doing this beginner project first, it will help you understand the basic layout and structure of a C# program.

To create a hello world program in Microsoft visual studio —the easiest-to-use Program possible, Select Create New project –> Console app (.NET CORE) and give the project a name. Since it is a simple program, call it helloworld.

Once you have created the application, it will contain a file called Program with a .cs extension. This indicates that it is a C# source code file. By default, it will contain some code that looks as follows.

```
using System;

namespace HelloWorld
{
    class Program
    {
        static void Main(string[] args)
        {
            Console.WriteLine("Hello World!");
        }
    }
}
```

A basic C# program has five core features. These features are:

1. Namespace
2. Class
3. Class methods
4. Main Method
5. Expressions

To run the code in Microsoft Visual Studio, select the Green play button in the Menu bar. Once the above Program completes compiling, the text "Hello World" will appear printed in a console window.

Let us look at the features of the above Program.

- `Using System`: This is usually the first part of a basic C# program. We use the keyword 'using' to include the System namespace in the included Program. For Java Programmers, this may interpret to the import packages or #include <header_file>. A larger program may contain more than one using statements.
- The second line in the Program contains the namespace keyword or declaration that contains a collection of classes. In the above Program, the namespace HelloWorld contains the class called Program – which by default is named after the name of the file containing the source code.
- The next line of the code contains the class declaration. The class contains the methods and the data definitions of the Program. It also contains more than one method used to define the behavior of the specified class. The HelloWorld Program above contains a single method called Main.
- Next is the Main method declaration. The main method is the entry point of all programs written in C#. As stated earlier, we use methods to define what the method does,

thus acting as the verb of the class. In this case, we used the method to print the text Hello World in the console. If you are familiar with Java, the main method looks like this.

```
public static void main(String[] args) {

    System.out.println("Hello world");

}
```

As you can see, C# borrows a lot from Java and C++.

- The last line of code is the Console.WriteLine() -This line of code is the action which is broadcasted by the method main thus printing the text inside the WriteLine() function.

NOTE: For the previous example, we used the Jetbrains Rider and the code may thus not have another code available in Visual studio. You may encounter Console.ReadKey() that causes the Program to wait for a key press before closing thus preventing the Program from executing and closing immediately.

C# Basic Structure and Keywords

Like most modern high-level programming language, C# has its constraints and rules that you must follow as you program. Most of these constraints are like those of its ancestors – Java and C++ but slightly different.

The following are some key points to note about C# programs.

- A C# program must contain a main method.
- Execution of a C# program starts at the Main method
- Unlike Java, the class name can be different from the filename containing the source code without causing any errors.
- C# is case sensitive and thus, the latter 'Class' and 'class' are two different words.
- You must terminate all C# statements with a semicolon

Those are the most basic and important rules in C# programming. Like other programming languages, C# also has specific keywords. In this case, and is the case with a majority of programming languages, keywords are words reserved and used by the C# compiler, and thus, you cannot directly use them as identifiers.

In programming, identifiers are unique words used to identify variables, classes, methods, and other data structures —we shall talk more about these in later sections.

The C# compiler reserves the following keywords for its use – different IDEs and text editors usually show them in different colors. However, you can use some of the keywords by adding the @ symbol at the beginning of the word. We do not recommend this practice.

NOTE: In C#, some keywords may have special meaning when it comes to the context of the written code. We call these contextual Keywords. Below is a table of the most common C# keywords.

void	explicit	break	using	decimal	continue	join
abstract	extern	else	enum	try	add	into
foreach	bool	sealed	case	event	unchecked	Gloab
interface	class	checked	for	out	base	group
as	ulong	do	if	sbyte	uint	
char	this	internal	in	randonly	alias	
while	public	operator	null	float	sizeof	
throw	stackalloc	int	in	namespace	ascending	
lock	private	unsafe	switch	struct	descending	
goto	true	long	false	set	from	

protected	const	out	ref	select	volatile	
implicit	new	finally	static	remove	dynaic	
ushort	object	override	typeof	delegate	get	
short	fixed	is	Virtual	orderby	let	
double	return	string	Params	partial	byte	

Comments in C#

Like most programming languages, C# allows us to use comments. The compiler ignores Comments and uses them to document the code for later use. Comments are very important since you can use them to refer to and explain the code if other programmers are working on it too.

You can create Comments in two formats:

1. Single line comments: We create single line comments using two forward slashes (//)at the end of the line
2. Multiline comments: We use Multiline comments to extend the comment to more than one line continuously. We create them using a single backlash and an asterisk and close them using an asterisk and a forward backslash (/* ...*/)

NOTE: It is always a good practice documenting your C# code by using comments.

C# Variables

In C# programming and most programming languages, Variables refer to a container used to store a specific type of data. A name given to a variable, also called variable name, is used to refer to the memory location where the variable is stored.

In C#, every defined variable has its specific type used to determine the layout and size that the variable can store. It is also used to define the type of operations that can be carried out on the defined variable.

C# has 5 main types of variables as shown in the table below:

C# Variable Type	Type Examples
Decimals Types	decimal
Boolean Types	True or false, as assigned
Integral Types	Int, byte, ulong, long, char, sbyte, short, ushort, uint, char
Floating Point	Double and floats
Nullable Types	Nullable data types

Variable Definition

The general syntax for declaring a variable in C# is:

```
<variable_type> <variable_name>;
```

Where the variable_type can be any of the valid C# variable types and the variable name is any relevant name you can create.

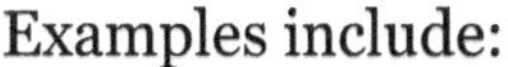

Examples include:

```
int age, price;

double currency;

char index;

float my_float;
```

In the above examples, age, price, currency, index, and my_float represent the variable name created by the programmer, while int, double, char, and float represent the data type of the variable defined by C# compiler.

Variable Initialization

You can initialize variables by assigning a valid expression or value. In C#, we conduct Variable initialization– to assign a value –using a single equal sign. The general syntax for variable initialization is:

```
<variable_type> <variable_name> = expression or value;
```

Example:

```
int age = 10; // value

double currency = 122.69; // value

float pi = 3.14159; // value

char index = 'A'; // value

area = 21 * 21 * 3.14159; // expression
```

NOTE: It is always a good programming practice to initialize values; otherwise, the Program may produce unexpected results.

Rules for Variable Naming

When naming a variable in C# and most of the programming languages, you must follow various rules. These rules ensure that no errors occur during variable declaration. These rules are:

1. Variable names can only contain alphabets, numerical values, and underscores.
2. Variable names cannot contain any special character except an underscore and @ symbol, which we use to name a variable after a valid C# keyword.
3. Variable names cannot contain a valid C# keyword unless otherwise.
4. No whitespaces between variable names; Join two words with an underscore or use Camel casing.
5. Variable names cannot start with a number

Below are examples of valid and invalid C# variable names:

Correct Variable Naming style

```
    class Program
    {
        static void Main(string[] args)
        {
            int age = 20; // plain text
            double _pi_ = 3.14159; //
            float @float = 129.59F; // using the @ for keyword variable rename
            char myChar = 'Z'; // using camel casing
            uint my_uint = 425697; // using underscore

            System.Console.WriteLine("Age: " + age);
            System.Console.WriteLine("Pi: " + _pi_);
            System.Console.WriteLine("Float: " + @float);
            System.Console.WriteLine("Char: " + myChar);
            System.Console.WriteLine("Unsigned Integer: " + my_uint);
            Console.ReadKey();
        }
    }
}
```

Incorrect Variable Naming Style

```
using System;
using System.Collections.Generic;
using System.Linq;
using System.Text;
using System.Threading.Tasks;

namespace HelloWorld
{
    class Program
    {
        static void Main(string[] args)
        {
            int 2age = 20; // cannot start with a number
            double float = 100; //cannot contain keywords
            float $myfloat = 10.45F; //cannot start with special symbol
            char my char = 'A'; // no whitespaces
            Console.ReadKey();
        }
    }
}
```

C# Data Types

In programming, we use Data types to specify the type of data that can be stored within a specific variable. We have already encountered various data types such as integers, doubles, and floats.

In C#, we have three main types of data types:

1. Value Types
2. Reference Types
3. Pointer Types

Let us look at these types in more details.

1: Value Types

Value data types are integer and floating-point directives, and can be assigned values directly as they contain direct data. They include int, char, double, floats. Value data types are derived from the System.ValueType class that is readily available in the C# compiler library.

As mentioned earlier, once the data type is specified during variable creation, memory is allocated to store values of that size and type. Value types can be broken down into more types such as:

- Predefined Value types
- User-defined value types

The following table shows the most common Predefined Value types provided by the C# programming language.

Data Type	Min Max Range	Memory Size
int	-2147483648 to -2147483647	4 bytes
float	1.5*10-45-3.4*1038 (7-digit precision)	4 bytes
double	5.0 * 10^{-324} -3.4 8 10^{308} (15-digit precision)	8 bytes
char	-128 to 127	1 byte
Signed int	-2147483648 to -2147483647	4 bytes
Unsigned int	0 to 4294967295	4 bytes
Signed char	-128 to 127	1 byte
Unsigned char	0 to 127	1 byte
short	-32768 to 32767	2 bytes
Signed short	-32768 to 32767	2 bytes

Unsigned short	0 to 65535	2 bytes
long	?9223372036854775808 to 9223372036854775807	8 bytes
Signed long	?9223372036854775808 to 9223372036854775807	8 bytes
Unsigned long	0 to 18446744073709551615	8 bytes
decimal	Minimum of -7.9 * 10?28 - 7.9 * 1028, with a 28-digit precision minimum	16 bytes
bool	True or False	1 byte
sbyte	-128 to 127	1 byte
byte	0 to 255	1 byte

In C#, you can use the size of the operator to return the exact number of bytes occupied by the variable. Below is a program to show the bytes size of the specified data types:

```
using System;
using System.Collections.Generic;
using System.Linq;
using System.Text;
using System.Threading.Tasks;

namespace SizeOfValues
{
    class Program
    {
        static void Main(string[] args)
        {
            Console.WriteLine("Size of int: {0}", sizeof(int));
            Console.WriteLine("Size of signed byte: {0}", sizeof(sbyte));
            Console.WriteLine("Size of byte: {0}", sizeof(byte));
            Console.WriteLine("Size of short: {0}", sizeof(short));
            Console.WriteLine("Size of unsigned byte: {0}", sizeof(ushort));
            Console.WriteLine("Size of unsigned int: {0}", sizeof(uint));
            Console.WriteLine("Size of long: {0}", sizeof(long));
            Console.WriteLine("Size of unsigned long: {0}", sizeof(ulong));
            Console.WriteLine("Size of char: {0}", sizeof(char));
            Console.WriteLine("Size of float: {0}", sizeof(float));
            Console.WriteLine("Size of double: {0}", sizeof(double));
            Console.WriteLine("Size of decimal: {0}", sizeof(decimal));
            Console.WriteLine("Size of bool: {0}", sizeof(bool));
            Console.ReadKey();
        }
    }
}
```

The given result from the above Program are below:

```
Size of int: 4
Size of signed byte: 1
Size of byte: 1
Size of short: 2
Size of unsigned byte: 2
Size of unsigned int: 4
Size of long: 8
Size of unsigned long: 8
Size of char: 2
Size of float: 4
Size of double: 8
Size of decimal: 16
Size of bool: 1
```

NOTE: The size in the above code is in bytes.

User-defined value types are data types created by the user as a way to ensure flexibility within the code. We can use this to illustrate the flexibility of the .NET framework programming languages. User-defined value types include:

- *Structures:* In C#, a structure is a user-defined value type that is similar to a class. Structures contain variables and functions similar to the C# native class. The main use of Structures is to store logically related values in a single definitive value type. Structures, on the other hand, cannot inherit from any class and vice versa. See the Program below illustrating C# structures.

```
using System;
using System.Collections.Generic;
using System.Linq;
using System.Text;
using System.Threading.Tasks;

namespace SizeOfValues
{
    class Program
    {
        static void Main(string[] args)
        {
            personal One = new personal();
            One.age = 10;
            One.firstName = "John";
            One.lastName = "Doe";
            Console.WriteLine(One.firstName + " " + One.lastName + " is " + One.age + " years old");
            Console.ReadKey();
        }
    }
    public struct personal
    {
        public int age;
        public string firstName;
        public string lastName;
    }
}
```

- *Constants:* Constants are normal variable types that cannot be changed. Values in a constant are assigned during the declaration and cannot be changed. Used for values that are not meant to be changed at any time during the execution. We declare them by using the keyword const in C#. For example, we can declare a variable such as PI as a constant since it cannot change – as long as you are on earth. `const int pi = 3.14159;` The code below will result in an error as we try to perform an operation on a constant value.

```
using System.Collections.Generic;
using System.Linq;
using System.Text;
using System.Threading.Tasks;

namespace SizeOfValues
{
    class Program
    {
        static void Main(string[] args)
        {
            const double pi = 3.14159;
            pi = pi + 20;
            Console.WriteLine(pi);
            Console.ReadKey();
        }
    }
}
```

1 The left-hand side of an assignment must be a variable, property or indexer

NOTE: It is always good to declare constant values in uppercase to differentiate them from normal variables.

- *Enumerations*: We use enumerations to represent a list of named integer constants where each constant is mapped to an integral value with the start index being zero. We normally use it when we need to define a fixed set of values from properties. The code below represents Enumerations that contain related constant values.

```
using System;
using System.Collections.Generic;
using System.Linq;
using System.Text;
using System.Threading.Tasks;

namespace SizeOfValues
{
    class Program
    {
        static void Main(string[] args)
        {
            Console.WriteLine(DaysOfTheWeek.Sunday);
            Console.WriteLine((int)DaysOfTheWeek.Sunday);
            Console.ReadKey();
        }
    }
}
enum DaysOfTheWeek
{
    Sunday = 1,
    Monday = 2,
    Tuesday = 3,
    Wednesday = 4,
    Thursday = 5,
    Friday = 6,
    Saturday = 7,
}
```

2: Reference Types

We use Reference data types to reference to actual variables in a program. They do not contain any actual data but memory locations of the variables they reference to. The relationship between the reference value and the actual value in the variable is direct. This means if the value in the memory location changes by either of the variables, the other variable automatically updates to reflect the new value.

Common types of reference data types include strings, objects, dynamics, interfaces, and classes – includes predefined and user-defined. Let us discuss some of these common data types:

A: String Types

We use the string type to create strong string literals in a variable. The string type is of the System.String class derived from object type. In C#, Strings are represented by enclosing them in double-quotes. Later sections of the book will cover String objects.

```
using System;
using System.Collections.Generic;
using System.Linq;
using System.Text;
using System.Threading.Tasks;

namespace SizeOfValues
{
    class Program
    {
        static void Main(string[] args)
        {
            string myName = "John Doe";
            Console.WriteLine(typeof(string)); // get the class of the string type
            Console.ReadKey();
        }
    }
}
```

B: Object Types

The object type is of the class System.Object class and is the root class of all data types in C# programming. Object types are very flexible, and you can assign to them a value of any type as long as you convert it appropriately. This feature of conversion from object to a certain type and certain data type to object is known as unboxing and boxing, respectively.

```
using System;
using System.Collections.Generic;
using System.Linq;
using System.Text;
using System.Threading.Tasks;

namespace SizeOfValues
{
    class Program
    {
        static void Main(string[] args)
        {
            int x = 200;
            object y = x; // Example of Boxing

            y = 200;
            x = (int)y; // Example of unboxing
        }
    }
}
```

C: Dynamic Types

Dynamic Types type came about after the introduction of C# version 4.0; their main use is to store any type of value. They help you avoid compile-time errors as the type checking of the data types occurs during run-time. However, you can get the type of a dynamic data type during runtime by calling the GetType() method off of it. The applications of the dynamic type are very massive as you can use them in methods due to the capability to accept any type of data as a parameter. However, in most cases, dynamic types behave like Objects. We create it using the keyword dynamic with a syntax shown below:

dynamic <variable_name> = value;

The Program below shows the use case of dynamic type and their respective type during run-time.

```
using System;
using System.Collections.Generic;
using System.Linq;
using System.Text;
using System.Threading.Tasks;

namespace SizeOfValues
{
    class Program
    {
        static void Main(string[] args)
        {
            // dynamic values
            dynamic @string = "This is a string type";
            dynamic @int = 100;
            dynamic @double = 3.141;
            dynamic @float = 3.14159F;
            dynamic @boolean = true;
            dynamic @character = 'X';

            // print the type
            Console.WriteLine("The native type of @string variable is: {0}", @string.GetType());
            Console.WriteLine("The native type of @int variable is: {0}", @int.GetType());
            Console.WriteLine("The native type of @double variable is: {0}", @double.GetType());
            Console.WriteLine("The native type of @float variable is: {0}", @float.GetType());
            Console.WriteLine("The native type of @boolean variable is: {0}", @boolean.GetType());
            Console.WriteLine("The native type of @character variable is: {0}", @character.GetType());
            Console.ReadKey();
        }
    }
}
```

```
The native type of @string variable is: System.String
The native type of @int variable is: System.Int32
The native type of @double variable is: System.Double
The native type of @float variable is: System.Single
The native type of @boolean variable is: System.Boolean
The native type of @character variable is: System.Char
```

3: Pointer Types

Pointer data types in C# acts as locators or indicators to a specific address of a value in the memory. In C#, Pointers perform similarly as pointers in both C and C++ programming languages. The following illustration shows how pointers work.

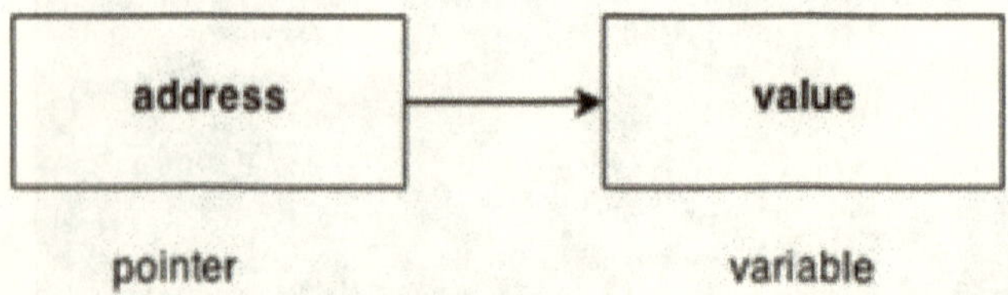

The general syntax for declaring a pointer data type is:

```
type* <address_identifier>

int* pointer;
```

To determine the address of a variable, we use the (&) and asterisk (*) to access the value of the given address.

NOTE: C# pointers and fixed-size buffers occur in Unsafe context, an advanced topic not covered in this C# guidebook.

In this section, we have covered the C# data types. Working with data types is very easy as long as you master how each data type works and its length. However, do not memorize the lengths, but it is good to know some of them. Keep practicing

Section 3

C# Type Casting

Type casting, also called type conversion, is a process of converting data types from one type to another data type. Type casting is very important and occurs in two different types:

1. Implicit Type casting
2. Explicit Type casting

Implicit Type casting

In C#, we perform Implicit type conversion in a type-safe manner. Examples of implicit type conversion are: conversion from smaller integral types to larger integral types.

Explicit Type casting

Users using pre-defined methods perform explicit type conversions using the cast type operator. Examples include conversion of double to an integer. Below is a program illustrating the use of explicit type conversion.

```
using System;
using System.Collections.Generic;
using System.Linq;
using System.Text;
using System.Threading.Tasks;

namespace ExplicitTypeConversion
{
    class Program
    {
        static void Main(string[] args)
        {
            double number = 7656.20;
            int numberDouble;

            // cast double to int
            numberDouble = (int)number;
            Console.WriteLine(numberDouble);
            Console.ReadKey();
        }
    }
}
```

Type Casting Methods

The following are the most common types of C# type casting methods.

Method	**Description**
ToInt16	Coverts the specified type to a 16-bit integer
ToInt32	Coverts the specified type to a 32-bit integer
ToInt64	Coverts the specified type to a 64-bit integer
ToDouble	Converts the specified type to a double value
ToBoolean	Converts a type to Boolean – if applicable
ToChar	Converts the specified type to single Unicode characters
ToByte	Converts the specified type to

	byte type
ToDecimal	Converts integers or floating-point numbers to decimal types
ToDateTime	Converts compatible types (strings and integers) to date-time structures
ToString	Converts the specified type to string type
ToType	Converts a type to the specified types
ToSingle	Converts the specified type to a small floating-point number type
ToSbyte	Converts the specified type to a signed byte type
ToUInt16	Converts the specified type to an unsigned integer type

ToUInt32	Converts the specified type to an unsigned long type
ToUInt64	Converts the specified type to an unsigned big integer

Now that we have covered the C# type casting, practice by trying to convert various data types to other data types and see if they are applicable.

C# Operators

In programming, Operators refer to symbols or special characters that help a computer program perform a specific operation on the given variables. Being a robust and efficient programming language, C# contains several types of operators.

They include:

- Arithmetic Operators
- Logical Operators
- Relational Operators

- Assignment Operators
- Unary Operators
- Bitwise Operators
- Ternary Operators
- Misc Operators

In this section, we are going to explore these operators' part-to-part. Let us get started.

1: Arithmetic Operators

We use Arithmetic operators to perform mathematical operations on supported data types. The table below shows the supported arithmetic operators. In this example, take x = 100 and y = 200

Operator Symbol	**Operation/Description**	**Example Operation**
+	Addition – add two values to give a single output	X + Y = 300
-	Subtraction – Returns the difference between second	X – Y = -100

	value from the first	Y – X = 100
*	Multiplication – Returns the multiple of two operands	X * Y = 20000
/	Division – returns the quotient of two specified operands	Y / X = 2
%	Modulo – returns the remainder of a division operation	Y % X = 0
++	Increment – Increases the value of the variable by one	X++ = 101 Y++ = 201
--	Decrement – Decrease the value of a given variable by one	X-- = 99 Y-- = 199

```
using System;
using System.Collections.Generic;
using System.Linq;
using System.Text;
using System.Threading.Tasks;

namespace Operators
{
    class Program
    {
        static void Main(string[] args)
        {
            int x = 100;
            int y = 200;
            Console.WriteLine("Addition: " + (x + y));
            Console.WriteLine("Subtraction: " + (x - y));
            Console.WriteLine("Multiplication: " + (x * y));
            Console.WriteLine("Division: " + (y / x));
            Console.WriteLine("Modulo: " + (y % x));
            Console.WriteLine("Increment: " + (y++));
            Console.WriteLine("Decrement: " + (x--));
            Console.ReadKey();

        }
    }
}
```

```
Addition: 300
Subtraction: -100
Multiplication: 20000
Division: 2
Modulo: 0
Increment: 200
Decrement: 100
```

2: Logical Operators

We use Logical operators to perform logical comparisons on given variables. The results of logical operators are Boolean types, i.e. true or false. The following table shows C# supported logical operators.

Operator Symbol	**Operation/Description**	**Example Operation**
&&	Logical AND – Evaluates to true if both values are non-zero or both expressions evaluate to true	True && True = True False && True = False False && False = False
||	Logical OR – Evaluates to true if either of the operands is non-zero or either of the expressions is true. The reverse is true	True || False = True True || True = True False || False = False
!	Logical NOT – Returns the reverse of the initial logical state.	!(True && True) = False !(False && False) = True !(True || False) =

		False

```
Console.WriteLine("----------------------LOGICAL AND------------------------");
Console.WriteLine(true && true);
Console.WriteLine(false && true);
Console.WriteLine(false && false);
Console.WriteLine("----------------------LOGICAL OR-------------------------");
Console.WriteLine(false || false);
Console.WriteLine(true || true);
Console.WriteLine(true || false);
Console.WriteLine("----------------------LOGICAL NOT------------------------")
Console.WriteLine(!(true && true));
Console.WriteLine(!(false && true));
Console.WriteLine(!(false && false));
Console.WriteLine(!(true || true));
Console.WriteLine(!(false || true));
Console.WriteLine(!(false && false));
Console.WriteLine("---------------------------------------------------------")
Console.ReadKey();
```

```
----------------------LOGICAL AND---
True
False
False
----------------------LOGICAL OR-----
False
True
True
----------------------LOGICAL NOT----
False
True
True
False
False
True
-------------------------------------
```

3: Relational Operators

We use Relational operators to perform relational operations on numerical values. See the relational operators supported by C# in the table below: Take x = 100 and y = 200

Operator Symbol	Operation/Description	Example Operation
==	Equal to = Returns true if the given operands/expressions	X == y = false

	are equal and false if not	
!=	Not Equal to – Returns true if the given operands/expressions are not equal to and false if they are equal	X != Y = true
>	Greater than – Returns true if the left-hand operand/ expression is greater than the left-hand operand/expression. False if not	X > Y = false
<	Less than – Returns true if the left-hand operand/expression is less than the right-hand operand/expression. False if otherwise	X < Y = true
>=	Greater than or equal to – returns true if the left-hand operand/expression is greater than or equal to the right-hand expression/operand	X >= Y = false
<=	Less than or Equal to – returns True if the left-hand operand/expression is less than	X <= Y = true

	or equal to the right-hand operand/expression	

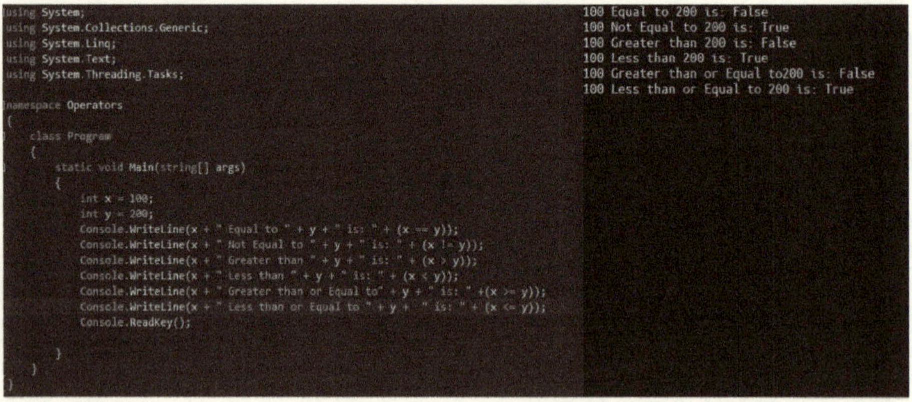

```
using System;
using System.Collections.Generic;
using System.Linq;
using System.Text;
using System.Threading.Tasks;

namespace Operators
{
    class Program
    {
        static void Main(string[] args)
        {
            int x = 100;
            int y = 200;
            Console.WriteLine(x + " Equal to " + y + " is: " + (x == y));
            Console.WriteLine(x + " Not Equal to " + y + " is: " + (x != y));
            Console.WriteLine(x + " Greater than " + y + " is: " + (x > y));
            Console.WriteLine(x + " Less than " + y + " is: " + (x < y));
            Console.WriteLine(x + " Greater than or Equal to" + y + " is: " +(x >= y));
            Console.WriteLine(x + " Less than or Equal to " + y + " is: " + (x <= y));
            Console.ReadKey();

        }
    }
}
```

```
100 Equal to 200 is: False
100 Not Equal to 200 is: True
100 Greater than 200 is: False
100 Less than 200 is: True
100 Greater than or Equal to200 is: False
100 Less than or Equal to 200 is: True
```

4: Assignment Operators

We use the assignment operators to assign the value of the right-hand operand to the left-hand operands. These operands could be raw data, variable, an indexer, or a property. The value assigned to the left-hand operands translates to the result of that specific expression.

NOTE: The data types of the right-hand operands must be compatible with the left-hand operand and corresponding operation. The table below shows the supported C# assignment operators.

Operator Symbol	Operation/Description	Example Operation
=	Simple Assignment – Assigns the value on the right-hand to the left-hand operands	x = a + b
+=	Add AND – Adds the value of the right-hand to the left-hand operand and result assigned to the left-hand operand	a += b is same as to a = a + b

-=	Subtract AND – Subtracts the right-hand operand from the left-hand operand and result assigned to the left-hand operand	a -= b is same as a = a - b
*=	Multiply AND – multiplies right-hand operand with the left-hand operand and result assigned to left-hand operand	a *= b is same as a = a * b
/=	Divide AND – divides the left-hand operand the right-hand operand and assigs result to the left-hand operand	a /= b is same as a = a / b
%=	Modulus NAD – Performs modulus on the two operands and assigns result to the left-hand operand	a %= b is same as a = a % b
<<=	Left Shift AND Operator – shifts the bits in the expression to the left by the number of positions in the additive expression.	a <<= b is same as a = a <<= b
>>=	Right Shift AND – Shifts the bits in the expression to the	a >>= b is the

	right by the number of positions in the additive expressions	same as a = a >>= b
&=	Bitwise AND – performs comparison on each bit of the first operand to the corresponding bit of the second operand with the AND condition	a &= b is the same as a = a & b
^=	Bitwise Exclusive OR – Compares each corresponding bit of the first operand to each bit if the second operand using the XOR condition	a ^= b is the same as a = a ^ b
|=	Bitwise inclusive OR – Similar to Bitwise XOR using the OR condition	a |= b is the same as a = a | b

NOTE: This book does not cover Shifts and Bitwise Operators. You can find more information about them in the C# documentation available here:

https://docs.microsoft.com/en-us/dotnet/csharp/language-reference/operators/bitwise-and-shift-operators

For the sake of simplicity, we shall not discuss the operators mentioned at the beginning as doing so may require knowledge about bit-by-bit operations and more.

5: C# Operator Precedence

Operator precedence refers to the order in which operators are performed. C# and many other programming languages require operator precedence to determine which action should be performed first, second, until the last in the case of more than one operator. Operator precedence is similar to the elementary mathematics formula BODMAS or PEDMAS. If the expression is solved in the wrong order, invalid and unrealistic results may be produced. In this section, we are going to look at which operator C# performs first and last.

Example:

Take an expression such as 7 + 3 * 10 – 16 / 8 + 100. This expression can have various results. If you type the expression in C#, the result will be 135. This is because the operators with higher precedence are evaluated first.

```
using System;
using System.Collections.Generic;
using System.Linq;
using System.Text;
using System.Threading.Tasks;

namespace MoreOperators
{
    class Program
    {
        static void Main(string[] args)
        {
            Console.WriteLine(7 + 3 * 10 - 16 / 8 + 100);
            Console.ReadKey();
        }
    }
}
```

The table below show C# operator precedence by category.

Operator Category	**Operators Included**	**Associativity**
Postfix	() [] -> . ++ --	Left to Right
Unary	+ - ! ~ ++ -- sizeof & (type)*	Right to Left
Multiplicative	% / *	Right to Left
Additive	+ -	Left to Right

<table>
<tr><td>Shift</td><td>>> <<</td><td>Right to Left</td></tr>
<tr><td>Relational</td><td>< <= > >=</td><td>Left to Right</td></tr>
<tr><td>Equality</td><td>== !=</td><td>Left to Right</td></tr>
<tr><td>Bitwise AND</td><td>&</td><td>Left to Right</td></tr>
<tr><td>Bitwise XOR</td><td>^</td><td>Left to Right</td></tr>
<tr><td>Bitwise OR</td><td>|</td><td>Left to Right</td></tr>
<tr><td>Logical OR</td><td>&&</td><td>Left to Right</td></tr>
<tr><td>Logical AND</td><td>||</td><td>Left to Right</td></tr>
<tr><td>Conditional</td><td>?:</td><td>Right to Left</td></tr>
<tr><td>Assignment</td><td>= += -= *= /= %= >>=
<<= &= ^= |=</td><td>Right to Left</td></tr>
</table>

In this section, we have learned the building blocks of the C# programming language. We have discussed the basic structure of a basic C# program as well as how each concept relates to the other in C#. Try to recreate simple programs of your own so that you can get a better understanding of the above concepts.

Section 4

C# Control-Flow Operations

In this section, we are going to discuss another important concept of the C# programming language. We are going to cover control flow operations that help us control how the Program executes based on certain conditions. To master C#, you need to understand variables and data types –discussed in the previous section.

Decision Making in C#

Decision making in C# and most programming languages allow the programmer to specify a certain condition to be tested in the Program. Once the condition is tested, the Program performs a task based on the result of the condition. The result of the tested condition is either true or false, where a different task is performed if either condition is true or false.

C# utilizes the following statements in decision-making:

- If statements
- If...else statements
- If...else if...else statements
- Nested if statements

- Switch statements
- Nested switch statements

1: C# if statements

This is the most basic conditional testing statement and performs an action if the tested condition is true. The basic syntax is:

```
if (condition) {
    //perform this action
}
```

Below is a C# program illustrating the structure of the if statements.

```
using System;
using System.Collections.Generic;
using System.Linq;
using System.Text;
using System.Threading.Tasks;

namespace ifStatements
{
    class Program
    {
        static void Main(string[] args)
        {
            int a = 200;
            if (a % 2 == 0)
            {
                Console.WriteLine("Number is Even");
            }
        }
    }
}
```

In the above code, the value of variable a is 200. In the second section, we are testing whether 200 mod 2 == 0. Since 200 is evenly divisible by 2 without a remainder, the condition is true and the text “Number is even” is printed on the screen. If you change the value of **a** to 101 or another odd number, the condition a % 2 == 0 will return false, and no code is executed.

2: C# if...else statements

The other decision-making statement is the if..else statement. The if else statement is similar to the if statement with the capability of performing an action if the condition is true. The general syntax is:

```
If (condition) {

        // perform this action if true

else {

        // perform this action is false

}
```

Let us modify the Program above to perform an action if the number provided is not even.

```
using System;
using System.Collections.Generic;
using System.Linq;
using System.Text;
using System.Threading.Tasks;

namespace ifStatements
{
    class Program
    {
        static void Main(string[] args)
        {
            int a = 200;
            if (a % 2 == 0)
            {
                Console.WriteLine("Number is Even");
            }
            else
            {
                Console.WriteLine("Number is odd");
            }
        }
    }
}
```

3: if…else if…else statements

This is a very common type of decision-making statement used to test for more than one condition. For example, we can test if the number is even or not. If it is even, then print “Even number”, else if the number is odd, print the remainder of the division and if not, print “Invalid number”. Look at the Program below.

```
using System;
using System.Collections.Generic;
using System.Linq;
using System.Text;
using System.Threading.Tasks;

namespace ifStatements
{
    class Program
    {
        static void Main(string[] args)
        {
            int a = 133;
            if (a % 2 == 0)
            {
                Console.WriteLine("Number is Even");
            }
            else if (a % 2 != 0)
            {
                Console.WriteLine("The remainder is: " + (a % 2));
            }
            else {
                Console.WriteLine("Invalid value");
            }
            Console.ReadKey();
        }
    }
}
```

4: Nested if…else if…else statements

We use Nested statements to check for checking multiple conditions using a single or close condition. For example, you can create a grading system that prints the Grade according to marks. For example:

- Greater than or equal to 80 – “A”

- Greater than or equal to 70 – "B"
- Greater than or equal to 50 – "C"
- Less than 50 – "D"

```
using System;
using System.Collections.Generic;
using System.Linq;
using System.Text;
using System.Threading.Tasks;

namespace ifStatements
{
    class Program
    {
        static void Main(string[] args)
        {
            int grade = 77;
            if (grade >= 80)
            {
                Console.WriteLine("A");
            }
            else if (grade >= 70) {
                Console.WriteLine("B");
            }
            else if (grade >= 50) {
                Console.WriteLine("C");
            }
            else if (grade < 50)
            {
                Console.WriteLine("D");
            }
            else
            {
                Console.WriteLine("Invalid Result");
            }

        }
    }
}
```

5: Switch Statements

We use the switch statement to perform an action based on a single condition. It is very similar to the nested if...else if statements. Switch statements use the case keyword when passing the condition to be tested.

The general syntax is shown below.

```
Switch (expression) {

case <condition>:

        // perform action;

        Break;

case <condition 2>:

        // perform action;

        break;

case <condition 3>:

        // perform action

        break;

...

default:

        // perform action if all cases are false;

break;

}
```

Each condition in the case statement is tested until one evaluates to true. If neither of the conditions are matched, the default condition is executed.

NOTE: Each case statement must end with a break statement to break out of the loop once the condition returns true.

6: Nested Switch statements

You can have more than one switch statement nested inside the other. It is also possible to have switch statements inside if statements and vice versa. In case of nesting switch and if statements, ensure that you end the loop or the Program will run forever.

C# Loops

In programming, we use Loops when executing a block of code more than once. Loops allow programmers to execute a set of code sequentially provided a given condition is true. Like most programming languages, C# allows us to utilize loops in our programs. The illustration below shows the structure of a loop in programming.

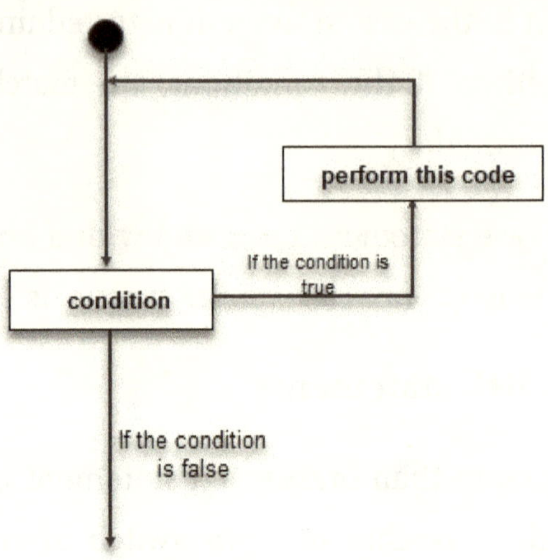

C# has two main types of loop statements and two secondary loop statements. They include:

- For loop
- While loop
- do...while loop
- nested loops

1: The For loop

The for loop is a statement used to perform a certain condition a specific number of times. C# for loop statement is very similar to that of C and C++. The syntax for the for loop is:

```
for (initialization; condition; loop_counter) {
//                    condition                    statement
}
```

The first step, initialization, initializes the loop that includes loop control variable declaration and initialization.

The second step, condition, sets the condition that the loop will use to evaluate which code will execute. If the condition is true, the code inside the curly braces executes. Otherwise, perform another action.

The third step is the loop counter. We use the loop counter to update the condition per each iteration. The loop counter utilizes the unary operators for loop update.

The following is a summary of how the for loop works

1. The initialization step runs only once.
2. The condition evaluates, and the loop body executes if it is true

3. Loops jump back to the loop counter and update the loop condition and run again

4. The process repeats until the condition becomes false and loops exits.

The program below shows how to use a for loop to print the first 10 numbers between 40 and 50.

```
using System;
using System.Collections.Generic;
using System.Linq;
using System.Text;
using System.Threading.Tasks;

namespace Loops
{
    class Program
    {
        static void Main(string[] args)
        {
            for (int a = 40; a < 50; a++)
            {
                Console.WriteLine(a);
            }
            Console.ReadKey();
        }
    }
}
```

On execution, the Program above displays the following result:

```
The value of a is: 40
The value of a is: 41
The value of a is: 42
The value of a is: 43
The value of a is: 44
The value of a is: 45
The value of a is: 46
The value of a is: 47
The value of a is: 48
The value of a is: 49
```

The for loop is very efficient when the number of iterations of the loop is known. If not, it is recommended to use the while loop.

2: The while loop

We use the while loop continually execute a specific code as long as the condition is true. The syntax for writing a C# while loop is:

```
While (condition) {

        // execute this code continually;

        // loop_counter;

}
```

Unlike the for loop, while loop might not execute even once. If the condition automatically executes as false, it skips the loop body. Below is a C# program illustrating the while loop.

```
using System;
using System.Collections.Generic;
using System.Linq;
using System.Text;
using System.Threading.Tasks;

namespace WhileLoop
{
    class Program
    {
        static void Main(string[] args)
        {
            int a = 40;
            while (a < 50)
            {
                Console.WriteLine("The value of a is: {0}", a);
                a++;
            }
            Console.ReadKey();
        }
    }
}
```

The output is similar to the for loop. If you change the condition to a number less than 40, the loop body will never execute since the condition is always 40.

3: The do...while loop

We have already seen that in the two already covered loops, the condition is checked before the loop body. In the case of a do...while loop, the condition is checked at the end of the loop body. This ensures that the loop body is executed at least once even if the condition is never true. The syntax for the do...while loop is:

```
do {

        // loop body;

} while (condition)
```

Notice that the condition is all the way down after the condition, thus ensuring that the loop will run once before exiting if the condition is false. On the other hand, if the condition, the loop will keep running and updating using the loop counter until it evaluates to false. The Program below shows printing the first 10 numbers between 40 and 50 using a do...while loop.

```
using System;
using System.Collections.Generic;
using System.Linq;
using System.Text;
using System.Threading.Tasks;

namespace doWhile
{
    class Program
    {
        static void Main(string[] args)
        {
            int a = 40;
            do
            {
                Console.WriteLine("The value of a is: {0}", a);
                a++;
            } while (a < 50);
            Console.ReadKey();
        }
    }
}
```

If we change the condition to a value equal to or less than 40, the Program will run once and print the value of a.

4: Nested Loops

Like most programming languages, C# allows us to create loops inside other loops. Nested loops can be a for loop inside a for loop, a while loop inside a for loop, do while loop and for loop, etc. However, when using multiple loops, adhere to caution to ensure they do not interfere with the program logic.

The syntax for writing a while loop inside a while is:

```
while (conditiion) {
        while (condition) {
                // code
        }
        // code
}
```

Nested for loop can be written as:

```
for (initialization; condition; counter) {
        for (initialization; condition; counter) {
                // code;
        }
        // code
}
```

Like other loops, we can also write a do...while loop inside a do while loop as shown:

```
do {
        // code
```

```
do {

        // code

} while (condition);
```

while (condition);

5: C# Loop Control

C# has loop control statements that allow us to alter the execution of a loop out of its normal execution flow. The following are the loop control statements available in C#.

1. break statement
2. continue statement

1: C# Break statement

We use the break keyword in a loop to break out of the current loop scope. If a break keyword is encountered in an inner loop, it only terminates the inner loop and passes the execution to its upper preceding loop. It is also used in the switch statement – discussed earlier.

The Program below shows the break statement after the value of a is updated up to 45.

```
using System;
using System.Collections.Generic;
using System.Linq;
using System.Text;
using System.Threading.Tasks;

namespace Break
{
    class Program
    {
        static void Main(string[] args)
        {
            for (int a = 40; a < 50; a++)
            {
                Console.WriteLine("The value of a is: {0}", a);
                if (a == 45)
                {
                    Console.WriteLine("Loop Terminated");
                    break;
                }
            }
            Console.ReadKey();
        }
    }
}
```

```
The value of a is: 40
The value of a is: 41
The value of a is: 42
The value of a is: 43
The value of a is: 44
The value of a is: 45
Loop Terminated
```

2: C# Continue Statement

The Continue statement is similar to the break statement, but instead of forcing the loop to terminate, it forces the loop to continue the iteration by forcing it to skip the code in between.

Continue statement in a while and do...while loop forces the loop control to move on to the conditional testing. In a for loop, the continue statement forces the conditional and loop counter to execute.

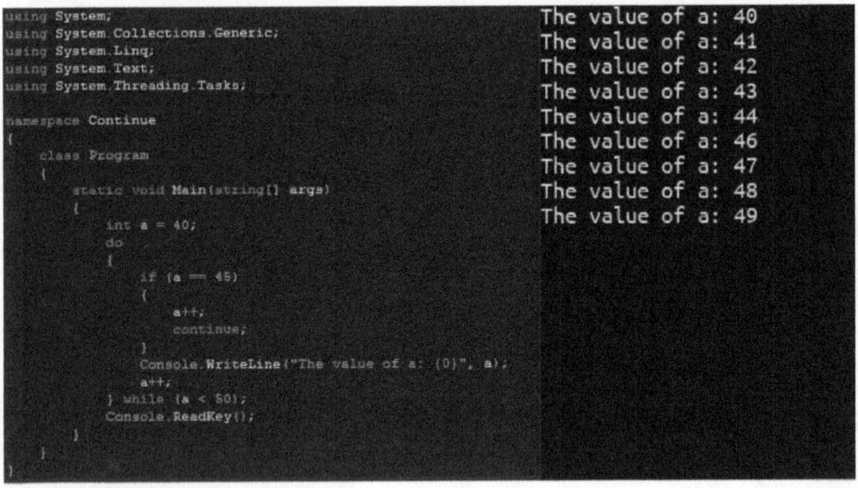

```
using System;
using System.Collections.Generic;
using System.Linq;
using System.Text;
using System.Threading.Tasks;

namespace Continue
{
    class Program
    {
        static void Main(string[] args)
        {
            int a = 40;
            do
            {
                if (a == 45)
                {
                    a++;
                    continue;
                }
                Console.WriteLine("The value of a: {0}", a);
                a++;
            } while (a < 50);
            Console.ReadKey();
        }
    }
}
```

```
The value of a: 40
The value of a: 41
The value of a: 42
The value of a: 43
The value of a: 44
The value of a: 46
The value of a: 47
The value of a: 48
The value of a: 49
```

6: C# Infinite Loops

Infinite loops mainly occur because of code but are sometimes created intentionally to consume a computer's processing power. We create Infinite loops by leaving the loop counter empty, making the condition always true and run the loop forever. Below is a for loop that never terminates.

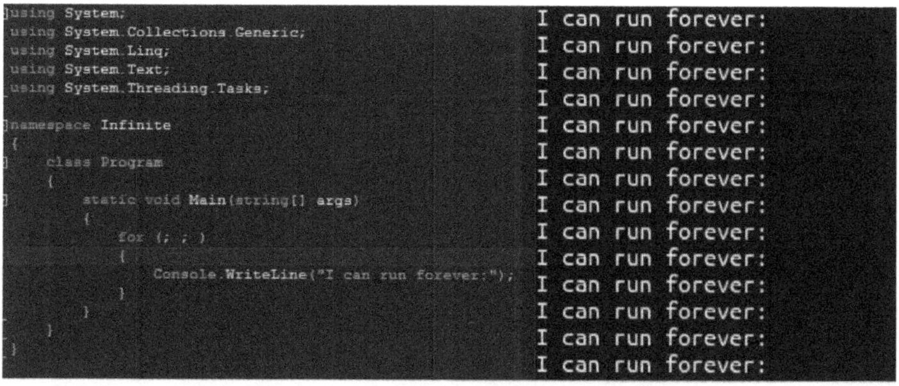

```
using System;
using System.Collections.Generic;
using System.Linq;
using System.Text;
using System.Threading.Tasks;

namespace Infinite
{
    class Program
    {
        static void Main(string[] args)
        {
            for (; ; )
            {
                Console.WriteLine("I can run forever:");
            }
        }
    }
}
```

```
I can run forever:
I can run forever:
I can run forever:
I can run forever:
I can run forever:
I can run forever:
I can run forever:
I can run forever:
I can run forever:
I can run forever:
I can run forever:
I can run forever:
I can run forever:
I can run forever:
```

As you can see, even without the Console.ReadKey() function, the Program does not close as it never stops executing.

NOTE: Some IDEs such as Intellij Rider will notice an infinite loop and warn you or automatically stop it.

We have completed the control flow section. Loops can be very hard to grasp at first but once you master them, they solve a lot of problems. Practice these concepts on a daily basis. Find solutions and fix them. That is the only way to learn. It may take some time, though.

Section 5

C# Methods

In programming, A method refers to a block of code with related logic used to perform a specific task. They are called functions in languages such as C++ and methods in languages such as Java. Every C# Program must contain at least one method called Main.

Methods are very useful in cases where you need to use one piece of code more than once. This makes the code remain clean, which in turn helps in debugging and improves efficiency.

In this section, we are going to cover how to use C# to create our own methods/functions.

Before you can use a method in C#, you need to undertake the following steps.

1. Define the method
2. Call the method

Method Definition

This is the first step to using methods. It includes using the correct structure of a valid C# method. The following parts make up a valid C# method.

- Access Modifier – We use Access modifiers to specify how the method will be accessed in the Program—for example, public, private, protected, internal, etc.
- Return type – The return types define the data type the method will return such as integers, strings, and void
- A function name – This is usually a unique name used to call the method when needed.
- Parameters – Parameters are arguments that we can pass during the method/function call.
- The method body – This is the logic of the method needed to perform the task of the method.

The syntax for writing a valid C# method is:

```
<Access modifier> <return type> <method name> (parameters) {

        // body

        // return value if available

}
```

We have already seen a method such as the main method in the previous programs.

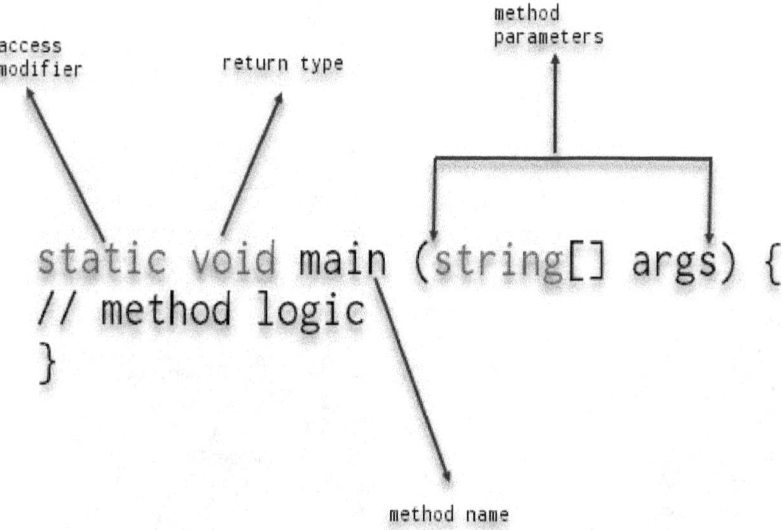

Let us look at an example program with a method to calculate the area of a circle.

```
using System;
using System.Collections.Generic;
using System.Linq;
using System.Text;
using System.Threading.Tasks;

namespace Methods
{
    class Program
    {
        static void Main(string[] args)
        {
        }
        static double AreaOfCircle(double radius)
        {
            const double pi = 3.14159;
            double area = pi * radius * radius;
            return area;
        }
    }
}
```

Method Call

After method declaration, you can use the method by simply calling the method name and then passing the necessary arguments. If you fail to pass the arguments required by the method, the program execution process will not complete. For example, to call the method AreaOfCircle, we pass the radius as the arguments as shown below.

```
using System;
using System.Collections.Generic;
using System.Linq;
using System.Text;
using System.Threading.Tasks;

namespace Methods
{
    class Program
    {
        static void Main(string[] args)
        {
            Console.WriteLine(AreaOfCircle(21.0));
            Console.ReadKey();
        }
        static double AreaOfCircle(double radius)
        {
            const double pi = 3.14159;
            double area = pi * radius * radius;
            return area;
        }
    }
}
```

In the above Program, we passed the radius of the circle when calling the method. In fact, we passed, the method AreaOfCircle inside the WriteLine method developed by C# developers. This means you can pass methods inside methods if the parameters match.

Recursive Method Call

Recursive method call is a concept where a method calls itself. Unlike a method call from another method, Recursive method call needs to be terminated using a termination condition. This helps to prevent the method from calling itself endlessly.

C# Parameter Passing

Methods with parameters require those parameters to be passed during the function call. There are three ways to pass a parameter during a function call. They include:

1. Parameter passing by value
2. Parameter passing by reference
3. Parameter passing by output

1: Passing by Value

Parameter passing by value is the default mechanism for passing parameters during a function call. This mechanism involves creation of storage space for each of the required parameters thus copying the actual parameters into the locations. The Program illustrates this mechanism by using a swap method.

```
using System;
using System.Collections.Generic;
using System.Linq;
using System.Text;
using System.Threading.Tasks;

namespace PassByValue
{
    class Program
    {
        static void Main(string[] args)
        {
            // locally defined variables
            int a = 100;
            int b = 200;

            Console.WriteLine("The value of a before swap: {0}", a);
            Console.WriteLine("The value of b before swap: {0}", b);
            // call the swap method
            swap(a, b);
            Console.WriteLine("The value of b after swap: {0}", a);
            Console.WriteLine("The value of b after swap: {0}", b);

            Console.ReadKey();
        }
        static void swap(int a, int b)
        {
            int temp = a;
            a = b;
            b = temp;
        }
    }
}
```

Once the above Program compiles, the following output displays.

```
The value of a before swap: 100
The value of b before swap: 200
The value of b after swap: 100
The value of b after swap: 200
```

This means that there is no change occurring in the values despite the values changing inside the function.

2: Passing by Reference

Parameter passing by reference involves passing the memory address of the actual variable. Unlike passing by value, the pass by reference method does not create new storage locations for the variables. In C#, we declare Reference parameters using the ref keyword. The Program below shows the usage of the pass by reference method call.

```
using System;
using System.Collections.Generic;
using System.Linq;
using System.Text;
using System.Threading.Tasks;

namespace PassByReference
{
    class Program
    {
        static void Main(string[] args)
        {
            // locally defined variables
            int a = 100;
            int b = 200;

            Console.WriteLine("The value of a before swap: {0}", a);
            Console.WriteLine("The value of b before swap: {0}", b);
            // call the swap method
            swap(ref a, ref b);
            Console.WriteLine("The value of b after swap: {0}", a);
            Console.WriteLine("The value of b after swap: {0}", b);

            Console.ReadKey();
        }
        static void swap(ref int a, ref int b)
        {
            int temp = a;
            a = b;
            b = temp;
        }
    }
}
```

Once the above code compiles, the output shall display:

```
The value of a before swap: 100
The value of b before swap: 200
The value of b after swap: 200
The value of b after swap: 100
```

This indicates that the values of the variables are swapping inside the swap method thus reflecting in the Main method.

3: Passing by Output

As we have already seen, we use the return keyword to return one value from a method. Using the output parameters, we can return two values from a function. Pass by output works similarly as pass by reference, except they do transfer data into the method rather than into the method. Since this method may be intimidating for beginners, you can find more information here. https://docs.microsoft.com/en-us/dotnet/csharp/language-reference/keywords/out-parameter-modifier

We have completed the Methods section. We have already covered topics such as method creation, method calls, and parameter passing. The best way to master these concepts through practice.

For example, if you create a program, try adding your code in another method and only call it in the main method. This will help you understand and become comfortable with Methods.

Section 6

C# Arrays

In this section, we are going to cover another important concept or data structure. Like most programming languages, C# allows us to create and work with arrays. Let us see what arrays are and how they work

We can classify Arrays as a group of related data that shares a memory location. We use Arrays to store a fixed-size sequential group of data of the same type. You can think of arrays as containers used to store variables of the same type in contiguous locations where the lowest location address stores the first element, and the highest address stores the last element.

For example, if we wanted to store 100 numbers, we can do it the basic way – creating variables named number0, number1, number2...number100. However, this is tiresome and consumes a lot of memory. Another way would be to create an array of 100 elements and access each element by index. Let us see how to do this.

Types of C# Arrays

Before we get into the code, it is good to note that C# has certain types of arrays. They include:

- Single dimensional Arrays

- Multidimensional Arrays
- Jagged Arrays
- Param Arrays

For the sake of simplicity, we are only going to cover single-dimensional arrays.

Array Declaration

To declare an array in C#, we adhere to the following syntax:

```
datatype[] array_name;
```

- We use the data type to define what type of data to store in the array.
- In the square brackets [] – the rank or the size of array is passed. It specifies how many elements will be stored in the array
- Array_name – specifies a unique name to identify the array. Always go for something creative but meaningful.

For example, you can use the following arrays to store integer, double, or character values respectively

```
int[] myIntegers;

double[] myValues;

char[] myChars;
```

NOTE: Once you declare the array, there will be no memory location created for it.

Array Initialization

As said, array declaration does not allocate memory. We need to initialize the array by creating an instance of the array. Since an array is a reference type, in C#, we use the keyword new to create the instance of the array. The syntax for array initialization is:

```
datatype[] arrayName = new datatype[size];
```

For example:

```
int[] myIntegers =  new int[100];

double[] myValues = new double[100];

char[] myChars = new char[26];
```

Value Assignment and Indexing

Once you have declared the array and it has initialized, we assign values into the array by using indexes. Array indexing starts at zero – this means if we have an array such as:

double[] myArray = new double[10]

The first number in the array is at index zero while the last element in the array is arrayLength – 1.

To assign values we use the syntax:

arrayName[index] = value;

For example,

```
using System;
using System.Collections.Generic;
using System.Linq;
using System.Text;
using System.Threading.Tasks;

namespace Arrays
{
    class Program
    {
        static void Main(string[] args)
        {
            double[] myArray = new double[10];
            myArray[0] = 10;
            myArray[1] = 20;
            myArray[3] = 30;

            Console.WriteLine(myArray[1]);
            Console.ReadKey();
        }
    }
}
```

Once you have assigned a value to the array index, you can use it by simply using its index.

NOTE: Unlike some programming languages such as Python, if You call the Console.WriteLine(myArray), the class of the array will be printed – in this case, System.double

Array Iteration – Foreach

We can access all the array elements using a for loop or a foreach loop. Since we have already covered the for loop, we are going to look at the foreach statement.

```
using System;
using System.Collections.Generic;
using System.Linq;
using System.Text;
using System.Threading.Tasks;

namespace Arrays
{
    class Program
    {
        static void Main(string[] args)
        {
            int[] myArray = new int[10];
            // initialize array elements
            for (int x = 0; x < 10; x++)
            {
                myArray[x] = x + 100;
            }
            foreach (int y in myArray)
            {
                int x = y - 100;
                Console.WriteLine("Element at index[{0}] = {1}", x, y);
            }
                Console.ReadKey();
        }
    }
}
```

Once the above code complete compiling, it will print each element in the array index. Since the for loop updates the array on each iteration, the array index does not repeat more than once. The output below illustrates that:

```
Element at index[0] = 100
Element at index[1] = 101
Element at index[2] = 102
Element at index[3] = 103
Element at index[4] = 104
Element at index[5] = 105
Element at index[6] = 106
Element at index[7] = 107
Element at index[8] = 108
Element at index[9] = 109
```

In this section, we have covered arrays and array operations. We have not covered Multidimensional arrays as they may end up being confusing especially if you fail to master single dimensional arrays. Ensure to master how to work with single-dimensional arrays before moving on to other types of Arrays.

Practice is the key to being a great programmer —whether you are programming in C# or in any other computing language.

Section 7

C# Strings and String Operations

In previous sections of this guidebook, we have used C# strings as characters. However, the best way to work with strings is by declaring a string variable and storing the string required in the variable. This allows for string operations and reuse of the same string if required.

NOTE: Strings are alias of the System.Class class in C# and we use them to store a series of characters.

How to Create C# String Objects

In C#, we can create Strings using various methods in. We have already worked with some of these methods. They include:

- Creating a string variable and store the string literal
- By using the string concatenation operator
- Using the String class
- Method call that the return value is a string
- Using a formatting method to convert the value or object to its corresponding string representation.

NOTE: We are not going to discuss the above methods one by one; instead, we are going to use a written program to illustrate how they work.

```
using System;
using System.Collections.Generic;
using System.Linq;
using System.Text;
using System.Threading.Tasks;

namespace Strings
{
    class Program
    {
        static void Main(string[] args)
        {
            // string variable
            string FirstName = "Jane";
            string LastName = "Doe";
            // string concatenation
            string fullName = FirstName + LastName;
            Console.WriteLine("Full name is: {0}", fullName);

            // string constructor
            char[] singleLetters = { 'H', 'e', 'l', 'l', 'o' };
            string complete = new string(singleLetters);
            Console.WriteLine("Jane: {0}", complete);

            // format method to convert value to string rep
            DateTime wait = new DateTime(2019, 11, 5, 22, 25, 1);
            string report = String.Format("Report delivered at {0:t} on {0:D} ", wait);
            Console.WriteLine("Report: {0} ", report);

            // method return strings
            string[] stringArray = { "Hello", "World", "C#", "Programmers" };
            string hello = String.Join(" ", stringArray);
            Console.WriteLine("C#: {0}", hello);


            Console.ReadKey();
        }
    }
```

Once the above Program compiles, it shall give the following output.

```
Full name is: JaneDoe
Jane: Hello
Report: Report delivered at 22:25 on Tuesday, 5 November 2019
C#: Hello World C# Programmers
```

String Properties

C# string class has the following properties.

- Length – We use the length property to get the number of characters in the specified String class
- Chars – We use this property to get the character at the given position in the String object

String Methods

We have a wide range of methods that are compatible with the string object thus allowing programmers to perform various operations on strings. These methods are many and we may not cover all of them.

1. Compare – We use the compare method to compare two strings and return an integer value to specify the relative

position sorted according to order. The syntax for this method is:

```
String.Compare(string1, string2, ignoreCase = true/false);
```

You may encounter methods that allow you to pass other arguments such as IgnoreCase that ignores upper and lower cases when set to true.

2. Concat – We use this method to concatenate two or more string objects to produce one string. The syntax for this method is:

```
String.Concat(string1, string2, stringN)
```

3. Contains – We use this method to return a Boolean value to indicate whether the defined string object arises in the string. The syntax for this method is:

```
String.Contain(value)
```

4. Copy – We use this method to copy a defined string by creating a new string object with the same value as the specified string. The syntax is:

```
String.Copy(string)
```

5. CopyTo – We use this method to copy the stated number of characters from a specific position of the String object to a specific position in an array of Unicode characters. The syntax is:

```
String.CopyTo(int SourceIndex, char[] target, int targetIndex, int count)
```

6. ToLower – When used, this method returns a copy of the specified string converted to lowercase

7. ToUpper – This method returns the specified string converted to uppercase.

8. StartsWith – We use this method to determine whether the start of the string instance matches the specified string literals.

9. EndsWith – This method determines whether the end of the string instance matches the specified string literals

10. Equals – returns a Boolean value if the specified string matches the current string object

11. IndexOf – We use this method to return the zero-based index of the specified character – specified character must be in Unicode Format – in the string object. There are

many variances of the IndexOf method each with different arguments

12. IsNullOrEmpty – returns a Boolean value if the specified string object is null or empty.

13. Join – We us this method to concatenate all the elements in a string array using the specified separator in between each element

14. Remove – removes the specified number of operators in the existing string object at the specified index position.

NOTE: This guidebook has left many string methods uncovered. Check out the C# documentation for more.

Section 8

Encapsulation

In programming, Encapsulation refers to the process of enclosing one or more items in a logical package. Encapsulation is a very important methodology of the object-oriented programming. It allows or denies access to implementation details of items in the Program by user-definition.

We briefly discussed elements of encapsulation in previous sections. In this section, we are going to cover it in more details.

Abstraction and Encapsulation are two aspects of object-oriented programming. Abstraction allows the visibility of items in the Program and encapsulation allows programmers to implement the level of visibility or abstraction of the items in the code.

We implement Encapsulation by using access modifiers – seen in previous sections. We use Access modifiers to define the visibility and the scope of members in a class. The class can be user defined or the pre-built classes. The following are the supported access modifiers in C#.

1. Public
2. Private
3. Protected

4. Internal

5. Internal protected

Public Access modifier

We use the public access modifier to allow classes to expose all its members —such as variables and functions – to other functions and objects from other classes. This enables other classes from the defined class to access these elements and modify them. You should only use the public access modifier when other functions can change the members of the class.

The Program below – used to calculate the area of a circle—illustrates this.

```
using System;
using System.Collections.Generic;
using System.Linq;
using System.Text;
using System.Threading.Tasks;

namespace PublicAccessModifier
{
    class Program
    {
        static void Main(string[] args)
        {
            circle Circle = new circle();
            Circle.radius = 21.132;
            Circle.displayArea();

            Console.ReadKey();
        }
    }
    class circle
    {
        // variables
        public double radius;
        public const double pi = 3.14159;

        public double returnArea()
        {
            return radius * radius * pi;
        }
        public void displayArea()
        {
            Console.WriteLine("Area of circle of radius: " + radius + "cm " + " is " + returnArea() + " square cm");
        }

    }
}
```

From the above Program, we declare the variables of the class Circle as public and are thus accessible from the Main() method. We do this using the instance of the circle class called Circle.

Methods such as returnArea and displayArea – which are in the class - can also access the variables without using any instance of the class.

Note that the declaration of the two functions inside the class circle is public and thus can be accessed in the main method using an instance of the class.

Private Access Modifier

We use the private access modifier to hide or restrict access of class members to functions and methods outside the declared class. This means that functions in the same class as the variables can access them. Instances of the classes do not have allowed access to variables.

```
using System;
using System.Collections.Generic;
using System.Linq;
using System.Text;
using System.Threading.Tasks;

namespace PrivateAccessModifier
{
    class Program
    {
        static void Main(string[] args)
        {
            circle Circle = new circle();
            Circle.getRadius();
            Circle.displayArea();

            Console.ReadKey();
        }
    }
    class circle
    {
        // private variables
        private double radius;
        private const double PI = 3.14159;

        public  void getRadius()
        {
            Console.WriteLine("Enter the radius of the circle: ");
            radius = Convert.ToDouble(Console.ReadLine());
        }
        public double returnArea()
        {
            return radius * radius * PI;
        }
        public void displayArea()
        {
            Console.WriteLine("The area of circle of radis: " + radius+ " cm is: " +returnArea());
        }
    }
}
```

When the above code compiles, the following shall be its output:

```
Enter the radius of the circle:
7.24
The area of circle of radis: 7.24 cm is: 164.674607984
```

In the Program above, we declare the members radius and PI as private and thus cannot be accessible inside the Main() method as they are not in the same class.

The methods getRadius(), returnArea() and displayArea() can however access the variables as they are in the same class. Since their declaration is public, they can be accessed in the Main() method using the instance of the class.

Protected Access Modifier

The protected access modifier allows the child class to access the member variables and methods of the base class. This helps apply inheritance and polymorphism.

Internal Access Modifier

We use the internal access modifier to allow classes to expose the member variables and methods to other methods and objects in the application. This means that members with internal access are accessible from any class or method with the application we defined.

NOTE: If you do not define the access modifier of the class members, the default access modifier is private. For example, if you do not define the access modifier of the class displayArea(), it is private.

Protected Internal Access modifier

We use the protected internal access modifier to hide members in a class from other classes apart from child classes within the current assembly.

Section 9

C# Classes & Objects

We have been mentioning classes for a while now, but we are yet to cover what they are or how they work. In this section, we are going to cover classes and discuss them in a way that allows you to know how they work.

In programming, Classes are blueprints for an object or data type. Classes do not define any data, but we use them to define what the objects of the class consists and the corresponding operations of the object. Objects are instances of classes. For example, A blueprint – a class in this case – of a car may contain the name, year of manufacture, manufacturer, speed, color, etc. It may also include operations such as ignite, brake, accelerate, repair etc.

Let us see how to declare classes and initialize them.

Class Definition

Creating classes in C# starts with the keyword class followed by the class name and curly braces to enclose the class body. To include an access modifier for the class, include it before the class keyword:

The following is a syntax for class declaration.

```
public class < class name> {

        // variables

        <access modifier> <data type> <variable name>

        // methods

        <access modifier> <return type> <method name>

                {

                        // method body

                }

}
```

The following are the most important points to note about classes and class members:

- We use Data types to represent the type of the variable
- We use the Return type to represent the type of return value of the method
- We use the keyword new to create an instance of a class
- We use the dot (.) operator with the instance of the class to access the class members.
- The access modifier specifies the access rules for both the classes and its members. If you fail to define it, the default access modifier for a class is internal while its members are set to private.

Constructors

A constructor is a special method with a class executed when an instance of a class is created. Constructors have same names as its base class but do not contain a return value. By default, constructors do not have parameters but parameterized constructors that accept supported parameters. Parameterized constructors help in assigning initial values to instances of the classes during creation.

```
using System;
using System.Collections.Generic;
using System.Linq;
using System.Text;
using System.Threading.Tasks;

namespace Constructors
{
    class Program
    {
        static void Main(string[] args)
        {
            circle Circle = new circle();
            Circle.setRadius(14.0);
            Console.WriteLine("The radius of the circle is: {0}", Circle.getRadius());
            Console.ReadKey();
        }
    }
    class circle
    {
        private double radius;
        public circle()
        {
            Console.WriteLine("Objected created");
        }
        public void setRadius(double rad)
        {
            radius = rad;
        }
        public double getRadius()
        {
            return radius;
        }
    }
}
```

Destructors

Destructors are also special methods of a class. However, they execute when the instance of its corresponding class goes out of scope. Destructors have the same name as its base class with a tilde preceding the name. Like constructors, they do not have a return value but cannot take parameters. They cannot be inherited or overloaded.

Destructors are very efficient at releasing memory before a program exits.

```
using System;
using System.Collections.Generic;
using System.Linq;
using System.Text;
using System.Threading.Tasks;

namespace Destructors
{
    class Program
    {
        static void Main(string[] args)
        {
            circle Circle = new circle();
            Circle.setRadius(14.0);
            Console.WriteLine("The radius of the circle is: {0}", Circle.getRadius());

            Console.ReadKey();
        }
    }
    class circle
    {
        private double radius;
        public circle()
        {
            Console.WriteLine("Objected created");
        }
         ~circle()
        {
            Console.WriteLine("Objected has been deleted");
        }
        public void setRadius(double rad)
        {
            radius = rad;
        }
        public double getRadius()
        {
            return radius;
        }
    }
}
```

Static Class Members

We can also define Class members as static. Once you define the member as static, this means only one copy of the static member is available no matter how many instances of the class are created. We can initialize Static values outside the member functions or inside the class definition. We normally use Static members with constant values as you can retrieve them by invoking the class without creating an instance of the class.

NOTE: You can also declare Methods as static, which can only access static variables. These types of methods exist even before the creation of an instance of the object.

Section 10

Inheritance and Polymorphism

Inheritance and Polymorphism is one of the most important concepts of Object-Oriented Programming. These concepts help with code reuse and implementation time. In this section, we are going to understand how to use these concepts in C#.

Inheritance

Programmers use Inheritance to define/create classes in terms of other class. Suppose you have a class that contains members and methods that are like a class you are about to create. Instead of creating new members for each class, you can choose to inherit the members of the existing class. The new class becomes what we know as a derived class while the existing class is a base class.

For example, a Mercedes is a car, therefore a Maybach is a Mercedes hence a Maybach is a car. This concept is what we call the IS-A relationship.

It is also important to note that you can derive a class from more than one class, and hence it can inherit member variables and methods from multiple classes.

The syntax for inheritance is:

```
<access modifier> <class name> <base class name>

{

        // body

}

<class name> <derived class name> : <base class name>

{

}
```

```
using System;
using System.Collections.Generic;
using System.Linq;
using System.Text;
using System.Threading.Tasks;

namespace Inheritance
{
    class Program
    {
        static void Main(string[] args)
        {
            Mercedes Maybach = new Mercedes();
            Maybach.setColor("Metalic Black");
            Maybach.setModel("SE-2019");

            Console.WriteLine(Maybach.returnInfo());
            Console.ReadKey();
        }
    }
    class car
    {
        protected string color;
        protected string model;

        public void setColor(string col)
        {
            color = col;
        }
        public void setModel(string Mod)
        {
            model = Mod;
        }
    }
    // derived class
    class Mercedes: car
    {
        public string returnInfo()
        {
            return "Mercedes: " + model + " " + color;
        }
    }
}
```

Once the above code is compiles, the output should be as the one below:

```
Mercedes: SE-2019 Metalic Black
```

NOTE: The derived class inherits all the variables and methods from the base class and you should therefore create the base class first – before you create the derived class.

Multiple Inheritance in C#

C# does not directly support multiple inheritance. To do this, we have to use interfaces. The Program below —used to calculate the price of painting a rectangular surface – shows the implementation of this concept.

```
using System;
using System.Collections.Generic;
using System.Linq;
using System.Text;
using System.Threading.Tasks;

namespace MultipleInheritance
{
    class Program
    {
        static void Main(string[] args)
        {
            Surface Rectangle = new Surface();
            int area;
            Rectangle.shapeLength(20);
            Rectangle.shapeWidth(10);
            area = Rectangle.surfaceArea();

            Console.WriteLine("Total cost to paint a surface of area: " + Rectangle.surfaceArea() + "cm2 is " + Rectangle.surfaceCost(area) + "$");
            Console.ReadKey();
        }
    }
    class shape
    {
        protected int width;
        protected int length;

        public void shapeWidth(int wid)
        {
            width = wid;
        }
        public void shapeLength(int len)
        {
            length = len;
        }
    }
    public interface Cost
    {
        int surfaceCost(int area);
    }
    class Surface : shape, Cost
    {
        public int surfaceArea()
        {
            return width * length;
        }
        public int surfaceCost(int area)
        {
            return area * 100;
        }
    }
}
```

```
Total cost to paint a surface of area: 200m2 is 20000$
```

Polymorphism

Object-Oriented programming has three core concepts: Encapsulation, Inheritance, and Polymorphism. We have already covered the first two. In this section, we are going to cover the last one – Polymorphism.

Polymorphism refers to existence of more than one form of an element. In programming, polymorphism means a variable of a supertype referring to a subtype object. Its main expression is as one "inheritance, multiple functions."

Polymorphism exists in two states:

1. Static polymorphism – in static polymorphism, method response is determined during compilation time. We call this early binding or static binding. C# static polymorphism is in two states:

a. Operator Overloading - Operator overloading refers to creation of user-defined operator-like functions. Overloaded operators are functions with the keyword operator and the symbol for operator definition following the function name. Like any other functions, they contain return value and parameters. Below is a section of a program illustrating operator overloading.

```
public static Circle operator+ (Circle a , Circle c) {
Circle circle = new Circle()
}
```

b. Functional Overloading – Function overloading refers to the concept of having two or more functions with the same name in the same scope. These methods however must differ in types and the number of arguments.

2. Dynamic Polymorphism – Determination of dynamic polymorphism occurs during runtime. Dynamic polymorphism utilizes the C# capability of creating abstract classes and virtual functions. Abstract classes provide partial class operations of interfaces, completed once a derived class inherits from it. The methods of an abstract class are also abstract and only applied by the derived class. Instances of abstract classes cannot be created nor can methods be declared outside and abstract class.

Virtual functions are in a class that you want to implement an inherited class. Since the calls of virtual functions are determined during runtime, you can apply them differently on different inherited classes.

Section 11

Interfaces

In programming, Interfaces are a logical contract between the inheriting classes and the interface. The inheriting class contains the logical how part of the contract while the interface defines the logical what part of the contract.

We can use Interfaces to define methods, events, properties that are members of the interface and they can only contain declaration of these members. The inheriting class handles the definition of these members.

Abstract classes can serve the same purpose when only the base class declares few methods, and the inheriting class is implementing the same functionalities.

Interface Declaration

In C#, we conduct Declaration of interfaces using the keyword interface followed by the name of the interface. Interface declaration is similar to that of class and public by default.

The code below is a sample interface declaration

```
public interface circle
{
    // members
    double radius;
    const double PI = 3.14159;
}
```

Section 12

C# Error Handling

Error handling is a very important concept that allows programmers to anticipate and handle errors in the Program before they occur. We also call it exception handling.

Like most programming languages, C# allows programmers to handle errors in programs. Let us cover these concepts briefly.

Exceptions allow programmers to transfer the execution control from one section of the Program to another. WE utilize exception or Error handling using three main keywords. Errors that occur in a program are 'exceptions.'

- try – Contains the block of code you are trying in order to t see if it runs with or without errors
- catch – this is the preceding statement after the try statement. It contains the block of code that handles the error triggered by the try statement. It indicates catching and handling the error
- throw – used in the Program to throw the error once it appears

- finally – This contains the block of code executed whether an error occurs or does not. For example, while opening a file, it must close whether an error occurs or does not.

Each of these keywords contains a block of code that runs if the condition is true.

If the try block produces an error, the method handles the error using try and catch block. The code inside the try and catch keyword is something we call protected code.

The general syntax for exception handling is:

```
try {

 // try this code

}

catch (ErrorName e1) {

        // perform this code

}

catch (ErrorName e2) {

        // perform this code

}

catch (ErrorName eN) {

        // perform this code

}

throw (e1, e2...eN) {

        // throw an error

}

finally {
```

```
        // perform this block no matter what
}
```

NOTE: You can create as many catch blocks as possible to handle different types of errors.

Exception Classes

Error handling exceptions in C# occur in their respective classes. These classes directly or indirectly derive from the main `System.Exception` class some of which include `System.ApplicationException` and `System.SystemException.`

The `System.ApplicationException` supports all the errors produced by the application programs and thus programmers derive their exceptions from this base class.

For system-based exceptions, they are from the System.SystemException class. The following are some of the common predefined exceptions derived from the `System.SystemException` base class.

- `System.IO.IOException` – used to handle all Input/output errors.
- `Syste.StackOverflowException` – used to handle all errors created from stack overflow.
- `System.DivideByZeroException` – used to handle errors resulting from a division by zero.
- `System.InvalidCastException` – used to handle errors produced during type casting
- `System.NullReferenceException` – used to handle errors occurring during null object referencing
- `System.OutOfMemeoryException` – handles errors produced to insufficient free memory

- `System.ArrayTypeMismatchException` – used to handle errors produced when type is incompatible with the array type.

a. `System.IndexOutOfRangeException` – handles errors produced when methods refer to an index out of array range.

Section 13

File Input/output Operations

In this section, we are going to cover file input and output in C#. A file is as a collection data stored in a computer using a specific name. For each file stored in a computer, we can use an absolute path to access it. A stream is a file that is open to reading and writing.

A stream is a flow of bytes that passes through the communication paths of a system. There are two main types of data streams:

1. Input stream – used to read data from a file
2. Output stream – used to write data to a file

These two types of streams help in reading and writing of files.

Input/output Classes in C#

C# has various classes used to perform file operations such as file creation, file deletion, read and write to files, and close files. The System.IO namespace normally maintains these classes. Commonly used file I/O classes under System.IO include:

- `File` – Helps in file manipulation operations
- `Path` – Used to perform operations on the path information

- `Directory` – used in directory structure manipulation
- `FileInfo` – Used to perform the supported operations on a file
- `DirectoryInfo` - performs operations on directories.
- `BinaryReader` – used to read original data in a binary stream.
- `BinaryWriter` – used to write the original data in binary format
- `DriveInfo` – Used to fetch information about the storage drives
- `StreamReader` – used when reading primitive characters in a byte stream
- `StreamWriter` – used when writing primitive characters in a byte stream
- `StringReader` – used for reading in a string buffer
- `StringWriter` – used for writing in a string buffer

- `MemoryStream` – used for random data access to the streamed data stored in the memory
- `BufferedStream` – used for temporary storage for a stream of bytes

FileStream Class Operations

We use the FileStream class contained in the System.IO namespace when performing file operations such as reading, writing, and closing files. It comes from the abstract class Stream in C#.

To use the FileStream class, you must create an instance of the class by creating a new file or opening an existing one. We use the following syntax to create an instance of the class FileStream.

```
Filestream <object instance name> = new Filestream(<filename> <Filemode.Enumerator>, <Fileaccess enumerator, <Fileshare enumerator>);
```

For example, the code below is used to read a file file.txt:

```
FileStream F = new FileStream("file.txt", FileMode.Open, FileAccess.Read, FileShare.Read);
```

The following are values of the parameters of an instance of object.

- File mode parameter values
- File Access parameter values
- File share parameter values

1: FileMode Parameter values

We normally use the FileMode parameter or enumerator to define the method for opening the specified file. These methods include:

1. `Create` – used to create a new file of the name specified.
2. `Open` – used to open an existing file of the name specified; you should give the Full path of the file.
3. `Append` – Used to open an existing file with the given name and append the cursor at the end of the file. It also creates a new file if the specified file does not exist
4. `Truncate` – Used to open a file and truncate the file size to zero bytes.
5. `CreateNew` – used to specify to the current operating System as to create a new file

2: FileAccess Parameter values

We use FileAccess parameter to specify the access mode of the file. The methods for this parameter are:

1. `Read` – opens a file in read-only mode

2. `ReadWrite` – opens a file in read/write mode

3. `Write` – opens a file in write mode

3: Fileshare Parameter Values

FileShare parameters contain the following methods:

1. `Read` – used to open files for reading

2. `Write` – opens a file for writing

3. `ReadWrite` – used to open file reading and writing

4. `Inheritable` – Used to allow the passing of inheritance from file handle to child process.

5. `None` – used to deny sharing of the file

The Program below shows the usage of FileStream class.

```
using System;
using System.Collections.Generic;
using System.Linq;
using System.Text;
using System.Threading.Tasks;
using System.IO;

namespace FileOperations
{
    class Program
    {
        static void Main(string[] args)
        {
            FileStream newFile = new FileStream("file.txt", FileMode.OpenOrCreate, FileAccess.ReadWrite);
            for (int i = 1; i < 10; i++)
            {
                newFile.WriteByte((byte)i);
            }
            newFile.Position = 0;
            for (int i = 0; i < 10; i++)  {
                Console.WriteLine(newFile.ReadByte() + " ");
            }
                newFile.Close();
            Console.ReadKey();
        }
    }
}
```

Step by Step

Console Calculator

In this section, we are going to create a simple console calculator that allows users to perform various operations on numbers. The code implemented by the Program encapsulates everything we have covered throughout thus guidebook and you can, therefore, practice what you have learned thus far by creating this Program. Since the code below has comments, we shall not discuss it part by part.

```
using System;
using System.Collections.Generic;
using System.Linq;
using System.Text;
using System.Threading.Tasks;
using System.Text.RegularExpressions;

namespace Arithmetic
{
    class Program
    {
        //validate the input to be of type double
        static bool InputValidator(string input)
        {
            string pattern = "[^0-9][.]";
            if (Regex.IsMatch(input, pattern))
            {
                return true;
            }
            else
            {
                return false;
            }
        }
```

```
//define arithmetic methods
static void add(double n1, double n2)
{
    Console.WriteLine("The Result is:{0}\n",n1 + n2);
}
static void sub(double n1,double n2)
{
    Console.WriteLine("The Result is:{0}\n",n1 - n2);
}
static void mult(double n1, double n2)
{
    Console.WriteLine("The Result is:{0}\n", n1 * n2);
}
static void div(double n1, double n2)
{
    if(n2==0)
    {
        Console.WriteLine("ALERT: Division by zero is invalid!");

    }
    else
    {
        Console.WriteLine("The Result is:{0}\n", n1 / n2);
    }
}
static void Main(string[] args)
{
```

```
string cmd = String.Empty;
do
{
    Console.WriteLine("Type help to get the list of commands available");
    Console.WriteLine("Type exit to exit the program");
    //command symbol
    Console.Write(":>");
    //make input as case insensitive
    cmd = Console.ReadLine().ToString().ToLower();
    switch(cmd)
    {
        //help command case here
    case "help":
    StringBuilder sb = new StringBuilder();
    sb.Append("start    Starts Calculator\n");
            sb.Append("exit     Exits Calculator\n");
            sb.Append("cls      Clears the Screen\n");
            Console.WriteLine(sb.ToString());
    break;
            //exit command case here
        case "exit":
            break;
            //start command case here
        case "start":
            {
                //take two inputs for the arithmetic operations
                Console.WriteLine("Enter two numbers:");
                string n1 = Console.ReadLine();
                string n2 = Console.ReadLine();
                //define two double variables for the inputs
                double num1=0.0, num2=0.0;
                //Filter the input for double data type here
                try
                {
                    if ((InputValidator(n1) == true) && (InputValidator(n2) == true))
```

```
    Console.WriteLine("Enter only numbers here!");
}
else
{
    //covert the input into a double data type
    num1 = double.Parse(n1);
    num2 = double.Parse(n2);
    StringBuilder sb1 = new StringBuilder();
    //arithmetic commands
    sb1.Append("add:Addition\n");
    sb1.Append("sub:Subtraction\n");
    sb1.Append("mult:Multiplication\n");
    sb1.Append("div:Division");
    Console.WriteLine("Type your commands here:\n" + sb1.ToString());
    Console.Write(">:");
    string choice = Console.ReadLine().ToString().ToLower();
    switch (choice)
    {
        case "add":
            add(num1, num2);
            break;
        case "sub":
            sub(num1, num2);
            break;
        case "mult":
            mult(num1, num2);
            break;
        case "div":
            div(num1, num2);
            break;
        default:
            //default command error message
            Console.WriteLine("Bad Command");
            break;
    }
}
```

```
                    }
                    catch
                    {
                        //arithmetic operation failure message
                        Console.WriteLine("ALERT: Something isn't right!");
                    }

                    break;
                }
                //clear screen command case
            case "cls":
                Console.Clear();
                break;
            default:
                //default wrong command message
                Console.WriteLine("Bad Command");
                break;

        }

        }
        //run the screen till exit command typed
        while (cmd.ToLower()!="exit");
    }
  }
}
```

We have completed our discussion of C# file operations. These file operations are very important and require a lot of practice to master. Keep developing programs so that you can test and practice the new C# skills you have learned. Practice is the only way to master C# and all other programming languages.

Conclusion

Thank you for reading this guide.

We hope that the guidebook has shown you just how easy it is to master C# once you master the core basics discussed in this guide; as mentioned severally, to become a better C# programmer, you need to practice as often and as consistently as possible.

The more you program and work within programs, the faster your programming skills shall develop, and the quicker you shall be able to create C# programs that provide real solutions.

Please leave a review for this book on Amazon by visiting the page below:

https://amzn.to/2VMR5qr

Your Gift

Let me help you master this and other programming languages quickly.

Visit

https://bit.ly/codetutorials

To Find Out More

www.ingramcontent.com/pod-product-compliance
Lightning Source LLC
LaVergne TN
LVHW041211050326
832903LV00021B/580

* 9 7 9 8 6 5 0 7 4 8 0 1 4 *